How to Have a Brilliant Career in Estate Agency

The Ultimate Guide to Success in the Property Industry

KATY M. JONES

COPYRIGHT © 2016 KATY M JONES
www.careerinproperty.co.uk

ISBN: 978-0-9957081-0-5
Edited by Danielle Wrate / wrateseditingservices.co.uk
Cover design by Rachel Su / rachelsu.com

This publication is designed to provide accurate and authoritative information for Estate Agents. It is sold under the express understanding that any decisions or actions you take as a result of reading this book must be based on your commercial judgement and will be at your sole risk. The author will not be held responsible for the consequences of any actions and/or decisions taken as a result of any information given or recommendations made.

CONTENTS

About the Author

Katy M. Jones successfully navigated a career as an estate agent. After 10 years as a residential and commercial negotiator, working for both independent and corporate agencies, she set up her own agency in London. After growing her business to a significant turnover, she sold it five years later for a considerable profit.

The Purpose of This Book

To provide a guide to anyone considering a career in the industry, whether they are school leavers, graduates or thinking of a career change.

The book provides a general introduction to the UK property industry and an in-depth analysis of careers in estate agency. Sectors such as new homes, surveying, property development and working in commercial property are covered. It looks at typical career paths within estate agency, qualifications for entry, the working environment, negotiating your salary package and commission structures, progression to management level and moving to a different sector within the industry.

JARGON BUSTER

General Industry Terms

Applicant - A person who is looking to buy or rent a property and is registered with an estate agent.

Valuation - A process whereby the sales or lettings manager or valuer evaluates the current market demand for a property and provides a sale or rental value. This typically involves an inspection of the property and takes into account its condition, location, features and size. The valuer will also consider recent transactions that have involved comparable properties.

Instruction - A property that is listed by the agent for sale or for rent, i.e. the owner of that property has 'instructed' the agent to market it for them.

'Signed terms or signed T&Cs' - Usually refers to the agreement between the property owner and the agent, with regards to their terms and conditions. This is signed off by the owner before they proceed with a sale or letting.

Energy Performance Certificate (EPC) - All properties available to buy or rent must have a valid EPC for the applicant to view before they commit to buy or rent the property. In practice, most agents organise for an EPC to be produced along with their photos and floorplan.

Properties built since 1st August 2007 will already have a certificate, which can be found on the central register. An EPC certificate is valid for 10 years.

OTE (On Target Earnings) - This is the amount you can expect to earn if you meet the targets set out by your employer. Be aware that an OTE figure is often an exaggeration of typical earnings, as the targets set may be largely unattainable.

Lettings Jargon

Landlord - The property owner who is letting out or wishes to let out their property.

Tenant - Someone who is renting a property.

Property management - The process of an agent managing a property on behalf of a landlord, usually because they have introduced the tenant.

Estate management - The process of an agent managing the maintenance, insurance and service charge collection for a block of flats in accordance with the requirements of the freeholder and leaseholders.

Tenancy agreement - A document, usually drafted by the letting agent, which confirms the terms agreed between the tenant and landlord. This is usually a standard document, which is amended to reflect the rent due, the terms of the agreement and the deposit paid.

Inventory/Check in – Refers to the process of an inventory clerk (usually an independent clerk as opposed to an agency employee or the landlord) visiting the property and creating a written and visual record of the condition and contents of the property, usually on the first day of a new tenancy. On the last day of the tenancy, a report is written to confirm the condition of the property at 'check out'.

Lettings renewal commission - When a tenancy continues after the initial period, usually 12 months, the agent may become entitled to a renewal commission, whether or not the tenancy becomes periodic (month-to-month rolling contract) or if the parties agree to a new, fixed-term contract. The commission depends on the terms agreed between the agent and the owner at the start of the tenancy. Many agents charge a renewal commission at a rate which is less than the first year, i.e. 5% in year two rather than 10% in year one. There may also be an administration fee due if an addendum, rent increase or new tenancy agreement is drafted.

Furniture package - A standard set of furnishings supplied by a tenant furnishing company, usually at a discount in comparison with a high street shop, with the convenience of the company installing all the items as part of the package. May include blinds, bedding, etc.

Deposit protection schemes - There are several schemes

available that the agent or landlord can utilise, including the Deposit Protection Service and the Tenancy Deposit Service. It's obligatory for a tenant's deposit to be registered with one of the accredited schemes. Some schemes hold the deposit, others insure the deposit held by the agent or landlord.

Gas & electrical safety checks – Every new tenancy requires a valid gas safety certificate to be in place before the tenancy commences. If no certificate is presented, the owner of the property or the agent is liable for prosecution, a fine and possibly a custodial sentence in the event of a fault with the gas appliances. The gas safety legislation is obligatory, so agents follow the regulations very closely. It's also recommended for the property to have an electrical safety certificate at the start of each tenancy, as the landlord is required by law to take reasonable steps to ensure the property is safe. In general, it's up to the owner to decide if they wish to follow the guidance or not, although some agents will insist on a valid certificate before a letting commences. Having the test done offers a degree of protection for the owner against the possibility of being sued by the tenant in the event of an electrical incident.

ERV (Estimated Rental Value) - This abbreviation is often used in the context of new homes.

Sales Jargon

Vendor - The property owner wishing to sell their property.

Buyer - A person who is looking to buy a property. This may be a first time buyer (FTB), a buy-to-let (BTL) investor or someone who is looking to buy a bigger property, a second home, move area or downsize.

IFA (Independent Financial Adviser) - Someone who can offer a range of mortgage products from a multitude of lenders, as opposed to being affiliated with a particular bank.

Property Misdescriptions Form (PMA) - A form the agent asks the owner of a property to fill in comprising an accurate description of the property, including any lease or service charge information, any rights of way and any guarantees with the property, etc. This is designed to help the agent provide accurate information to prospective buyers. It also protects the agent from being sued if the owner wrongly describes the property.

Freehold – The legal title that comes with a building that you own in its entirety. Most houses are freehold, which means you own the ground that it's built on, along with the walls and roof space.

Leasehold - This usually comes into play when the property is divided into flats. There will be a 'freeholder' who owns the building, and each leaseholder is granted a lease that gives them the right to occupy a part of the building for a fixed period of time, usually 125 or 99 years.

Leasehold with Share of Freehold – The building's freehold is shared between the leaseholders. This means there is no independent freeholder.

Service charges and ground rent - If you have a leasehold property, you will be required to pay towards the costs of insuring the building as well as maintenance and repairs. You will also pay a ground rent to the freeholder. Typically, this will be an amount of £100 to £300. The figure will be set out in the property's lease.

Sales memorandum - A document drafted by the agent when a sale is agreed. It sets out the parties to the sale (the buyer, vendor and their respective solicitors), the property address, the council borough where the property is situated and any special terms agreed between the two parties.

Exchange of Contracts – This is the point in the process of a sale where both buyer and seller have entered into a legally binding contract under which the buyer agrees to buy the house and the seller agrees to sell it. The contracts set out the terms of the sale, such as the price and completion date.

Completion – This is the final stage in the sale of a property and refers to the point at which it legally changes ownership. The process of 'exchange' and 'completion' are handled by the solicitors acting for the buyer and the vendor.

Industry Qualifications

NAEA (National Association of Estate Agents) - A group that sets out certain standards of operation for its members and offers training courses (part of NFoPP).

ARLA (Association of Residential Letting Agents) - As above but for letting agents (part of NFoPP).

NFoPP - National Federation of Property Professionals.

CHAPTER 1

BACKGROUND TO THE INDUSTRY, OFFICE STRUCTURE AND TYPICAL AGENCY SETUP

According to the Office for National Statistics, the estate agency industry is one of the fastest growing industries in the UK. In 2013, the number of people working in this sector soared to 562,000, an increase of 77,000 new workers within a single year.

So, what's the appeal? A major factor for university and college leavers, as well as for those changing careers, is the ease of entry into the industry for all levels of education and experience. There are no specific qualification barriers, there is the prospect of a higher starting salary than in many other industries, and there are good long-term career prospects. In addition, as there are at least a handful of estate agents in every major town and city, it's possible to find work across the whole of the UK. However, this is not a job for the faint-hearted. It demands long hours, including evenings and weekends, there is constant pressure to sell or let and you will be required to deal with the day-to-day stress that naturally arises from the process of moving itself. Most people find moving home stressful and if, for example, you are handling 10 sales at any one time, each with a buying couple and a selling couple, their solicitors, various school and holiday deadlines and the odd divorce thrown into the mix, you will quickly find that your phone rings constantly and your personal anxiety levels will start to reflect those of your clients.

Some people thrive in this environment and find it hugely stimulating and rewarding, while others rapidly sink under the pressure from clients, bosses and targets, only managing to stay in the industry for a few months.

The following pages will help you decide whether the industry is right for you and, if it is, choose between the various sectors comprising sales, lettings, new homes and commercial property. It will also show you the type of agency to aim for.

During my time as an employer, I interviewed a multitude of prospective candidates, many of whom had no previous experience in the industry. During the course of these interviews, it often became clear that the would-be employees knew very little of what the job really entailed - be that a role in sales, lettings, property management or administration.

The roles within a typical estate agency office are very well defined and include the following:

Branch manager

They will oversee sales and lettings. If the office is big enough, there might be separate managers for the two areas.

A branch manager typically oversees the running of the office to ensure targets are met. They supervise negotiations, carry out valuations (unless there is a separate valuations manager) and keep an eye on the progression of the sales or lettings process, which is usually undertaken by negotiators. They also ensure the legal requirements of business processes are met, deal with HR, training and recruitment, and report to the business owner or, if it is a larger group, the Area Director.

Negotiators

There will be a number of negotiators dealing with either sales or lettings. Their job is to book and undertake viewings, receive and negotiate offers, and deal with vendors and landlords.

Office administrator

Many estate agents have an office administrator, but what their job entails can vary widely. Usual activities include uploading photographs and drafting property descriptions, drafting tenancy agreements and sales memorandums (these detail the various parties to a sale, including the buyer, the vendor and their respective solicitors, along with the terms of the sale). The administrator may also coordinate the tenancy move ins, carrying out reference checks and registering deposits. In smaller offices, their role may include some property management duties, such as checking that rents have been paid or organising basic property repairs.

Other administrative duties include ordering office supplies and, in some cases, taking property photos and drawing up floorplans. Although it's not considered to be a senior position in the office, the role of the administrator is essential to the smooth, day-to-day running of the business and, ultimately, its profitability. Without an effective administrator, an office can quickly generate a backlog of paperwork, which will distract the sales and lettings teams from their principal activities and consequently reduce the number of new sales or lettings agreed.

In an agency with just one single office, many tasks will be shared between colleagues. This gives someone who is newly entering the industry a good range of experience in the overall business. In larger, multi-office agencies, the roles become increasingly differentiated. For instance, a lettings negotiator will never be asked to take photos of a property, as there will be a professional photographer assigned to this task. There's also less likelihood of an administrator in each office, as the carrying out of tenancy agreements and property management duties will be coordinated from a centralised office. This saves on costs and enables a far greater volume of services to be delivered. However, this will, in turn, reduce the range of experience gained by a negotiator.

Most estate agency businesses offer both sales and lettings services from the same office. This is because the two sectors complement one another and it increases the opportunity for business to be referred from one department to another. Equally, new homes and mortgage advisers offer complementary services that can generate multiple income streams for the business.

The following is an example of how the departments can interact.

A prospective buyer walks into the office to enquire about a new build property. They are looking to buy the property as a rental investment and will need to arrange a buy-to-let mortgage. As well as speaking to the new homes sales person about the property, the buyer wishes to have a rental valuation carried out. The new homes salesperson calls over their lettings colleague, who provides an estimated rental valuation, along with advice on furnishings, etc. The new homes salesperson then offers the buyer the possibility of a quick chat with the in-house financial adviser, who provides a mortgage quotation based on the estimated rental valuation, giving the buyer confidence to make an offer, which is accepted. The sale proceeds and a few months later the lettings department finds a tenant for the property. The property management team takes care of rent collection and the property's upkeep.

Two years on, the new owner decides to sell the property, and the agency receives the sales instruction. In this situation, the office is receiving a fee from the developer to sell the new build property, a fee from the mortgage lender for introducing the new mortgagee, a fee from the new owner to let and manage the property and a fee from the owner, albeit two years later, to sell the property again. They may also receive a fee by recommending a solicitor to the buyer or vendor and even for referring the buyer to an interior furnishing company for buying the furniture included in the let.

It is, therefore, essential that whatever the size of the agency, the different departments of the business remain connected. The ideal office environment will be one where all the employees are motivated to make as many inter-department referrals as possible.

FAQ 1. Sex differentiation in job roles

'*Is it true that sales is a male-dominated domain and lettings is more popular with women?*'

Answer: Yes and no. When I worked for one of the larger chains of agents in South West London, there were 12 staff members in the office. The lettings team comprised four females, including a female lettings manager, and a single male lettings negotiator. The sales team consisted of four males, including the sales manager, and me. I was the sole female on the sales team. There was also a female administrator and a male IFA.

This is quite a typical situation within the industry. However, there are no real barriers to entering either the sales or lettings side of the industry for either sex. In either sector, both sexes are well represented.

There is, however, a marked decrease in the number of female senior managers and directors. In my opinion, this reflects the general pattern across many UK industries as women take a break from work to raise a family. There is no real obstacle for women wanting to become a director, providing they have the right skillset. At the time of writing, the Group CEO of Countrywide (the largest estate agency group in the UK) is Alison Platt. Her experience has been gained through running large corporations rather than from climbing the ranks of the estate agency world, but nonetheless this should be seen as a very encouraging sign for all ambitious women entering the industry.

CHAPTER 2

JOB HUNTING: ENTRY ROUTES, UNDERSTANDING ROLES AND SALARY EXPECTATIONS

There are a multitude of entry routes into the industry. Most agencies will use a recruitment company to help find suitable candidates to fill their vacancies. Often, agencies prefer to promote existing staff to higher levels and recruit new staff into more junior roles. This process of rising through the ranks has several advantages for the agency. Firstly, the recruitment costs (recruitment fees, company cars, etc.) for a junior negotiator are much less than for a manager or director. Rising through the ranks helps to strengthen a company's culture, as less experienced staff don't bring as much baggage or as many bad habits from their previous roles, and they can be more easily moulded into the company's preferred processes. Something else to consider regarding the benefits of promoting from within is how high staff turnover can be. The cost to recruit and train a junior negotiator to manager level runs into the tens of thousands of pounds. Internal promotion is the best way to retain experienced employees. Despite this preference, a quick search through a recruitment agency's postings will reveal a wide range of vacancies at all levels, from director to junior negotiator.

As well as providing a major entry route into the industry, recruitment agencies can also be a very useful advisory service to less experienced job hunters. Several recruitment companies specialise in estate agency and property roles. Consequently, they are experts in the culture of different agencies and will be able to educate you on their working conditions and the salary expectations for each available role. Some will pre-interview job applicants for a role. Or, as part of their registration process, they may, for example, help applicants decide whether sales or lettings are a better fit for their skills and personality.

The larger agencies, such as Savills, DTZ or CBRE, may look to recruit graduates directly from certain universities, particularly those leaving with commercial property, surveying or estate management qualifications. In recent years, estate agents have frequently looked to recruit degree-qualified applicants for negotiator positions. However, in general, the industry is not particularly hung up on employees being educated to a certain level, or on them having a degree in a particular field. Personality, sales ability and ambition have always been highly rated too. A good level of written and spoken English and maths is considered essential, along with competence in IT. This is because the job involves using computerised databases for day-to-day work processes within the office.

Recommendations and personal introductions also feature as a means of finding employment, and companies will happily consider applicants who come to them direct. There remains the option of dropping your CV and a letter of introduction to agencies within the area where you are seeking work, although this can be hit and miss and involves a lot of leg work.

FAQ 2. Ageism in Estate Agency

'Why are there proportionately more younger negotiators, and are there barriers in place for prospective employees who are older?'

Answer: It's true that the majority of junior negotiators fall into the 20 to 30-age bracket. At entry level, most negotiators will be working very long hours – frequently 8.30am to 7pm or 8pm and every Saturday from 9am to 5pm, often without time off in lieu. Some offices even open on Sundays. In fact, holidays are limited, with some agencies offering 20 days annual leave per year, including bank holidays. If the agency closes between Christmas and New Year and forces staff to take some of their allocated days during this period, vacation time can effectively be reduced further, to just two-and-a-half weeks. Basic salaries are also low, starting at £10,000-15,000 per annum, with a further £10,000-15,000 in commission if targets are met. As well as being a pressurised sales job, with constant phone calls, emails and demands from clients, team members and bosses, the average negotiator will undertake 30 to 40 viewings per week. That requires a lot of running around, driving, parking, door opening and dashing back to the office for the next client. Physically, it's quite a demanding job. The junior negotiator role therefore fits the younger staff members who maybe have lower day-to-day living costs, as they don't have a family to feed. They may also thrive in the work hard, play hard environment and have the physical and mental energy required to profit from the pace of work. Any pitfalls to having a younger team? Yes. There are cases of junior negotiators calling in sick on a Saturday after their big Friday night out.

Is it a good idea to recruit older people, i.e. 40+ for junior negotiator roles? Absolutely, YES! I have done so in my own business. Older negotiators naturally command more respect from buyers and tenants. Many will assume they are more senior and will be more comfortable dealing with them than a 20 year old. They will also bring a whole range of life skills to the table, and many will have bought and sold or moved home multiple times. They may even have their own buy-to-let investments. This brings credibility and a huge boost to client-agency relations.

Did I find they were able to keep up the pace with viewings? Mostly, yes, and they also became more selective with their appointments and subsequently more effective. Were there any pitfalls to employing older negotiators? Yes, bad habits were often brought from previous employment situations, and there tended to be a lack of aptitude for IT if their previous role hadn't utilised it. In my opinion, the industry would greatly benefit from a more balanced age range in the office. However, in order to find this new balance, the employment conditions for junior negotiators would have to change sufficiently in order to appeal to older workers.

Roles, skillsets and salaries

ROLE: Junior Sales/Lettings Negotiator

SKILLSET: Good level of spoken/written English, basic maths, sales ability, good timekeeping and good teamwork skills. Quick learner, good memory for names and faces, likeable and good general people skills. Confidence to handle buyers and tenants who are often working in senior roles themselves, along with common sense. Ability to multi-task and prioritise, and to thrive under pressure. Self-motivated and determined enough to meet and exceed targets. Physically fit and energetic, so can cope with rushing from one appointment to the next. Genuine interest in property, enjoys dealing with customers and closing deals! I have not included negotiation skills, which are rarely found in a new junior negotiator, but can quickly be taught by a manager or through on-the-job experience.

SALARY: Base salary £10-15K + commission OTE £20-40K

ROLE: Senior Negotiator Sales/Lettings

SKILLSET: As above, with the addition of 18 months to three years industry experience. Experienced viewer and able to close transactions single-handedly. Competent negotiator able to manage vendor/landlord relationships. Has completed all compliance and business process training, understands the sales/lettings process in detail and can answer the majority of vendor/landlord questions. May have completed an entry-level NAEA or ARLA qualification. Has accompanied the sales/lettings manager on several valuations and may be able to undertake a valuation singlehandedly if required. Able to assist in the day-to-day running of the office and help train junior staff members. A more experienced senior negotiator will be competent enough to run the office when the sales or lettings manager is on holiday.

SALARY: Base of £15-20K + commission OTE £30-60K

ROLE: Administrator

SKILLSET: Must possess a high level of written English, along with excellent organisational skills. They need to enjoy organising files and completing checklists. This person must also be confident enough to pick up the phone and politely chase up missing paperwork from landlords and vendors. Although they will be working as part of a team, they must be self-motivated and support the sales and lettings teams' workflow to help maximise profits. An experienced administrator should be competent in all areas of the sales and lettings processes. On the lettings side, they should be adept at drafting tenancy agreements and organising the various paperwork requirements of a new letting. For example, taking ID, running reference checks, organising an inventory/check in, requesting and confirming the receipt of rent monies, registering tenancy deposits, executing tenancy agreements and ensuring gas and electrical safety requirements are met. On the sales side, they should be competent in drafting sales memorandums and their accompanying letters. They may be asked to write property descriptions, updating the details on the company websites and various property portals. They may also prepare, send and chase up sales and lettings invoices.

SALARY: Fixed salary of £18-25K, depending on experience.

ROLE: Sales/Lettings Manager

SKILLSET: Must be highly capable at staff management and able to recruit, train, motivate and direct a team of around three to eight negotiators, along with an administrator. Secondly, the manager must be extremely good at generating new instructions (when a property owner 'instructs' the agency to commence marketing their property, this is referred to as a new instruction). The overall skills required are much the same whether they are a sales or lettings manager, however, the processes and tactics employed to get from sales instruction to completion, or lettings instruction to the tenants actually moving in, will be different.

SALARY: Base of £20-25K + commission OTE £35-100K

ROLE: Valuer

SKILLSET: In the majority of offices, property valuations are carried out by sales or lettings managers. However, in larger organisations, there will often be a dedicated valuer. They will be hired when the volume of valuations in a particular office is too high to be undertaken by the managers. In this case, the valuer's sole activity will be to generate new instructions for the office. Core skills include being excellent at building rapport, i.e. they can gain the trust of new clients so that they will award them the instruction. They must also have a good long-term memory for names, faces and properties, as some clients may come back after a six-month period wishing to instruct them. This should be considered a relatively senior role within the office, since gaining a new instruction is the start of the revenue process and demands someone with excellent people skills as well as local knowledge. Most valuers will have at least two to three years industry experience.

SALARY: Base of £20-25K + commission OTE £35-50K

ROLE: Mortgage Adviser

SKILLSET: This person will often be employed by an associated company. They will have trained to become a mortgage adviser and completed a CeMAP qualification. Most advisers will be IFAs (Independent Financial Advisers), so they won't work for any one bank in particular and will be able to offer advice on a range of products from various lending groups. They will work very closely with the sales team, helping prospective buyers to understand their potential purchasing budget, and later arranging finance on their purchase once they have agreed a sale. Good people skills are essential, as are sales skills, as it is, at its most basic level, a sales job.

SALARY: Base of £20-30K plus commission OTE £35-50K

ROLE: Property Manager

SKILLSET: The key skills here are patience, a calm temper, a positive attitude, problem-solving aptitude and great organisational skills. A successful property manager will have good general life experience and common sense and a decent understanding of common property problems and how best to avoid and resolve them. They will be able to handle stressed and angry tenants and landlords, and be superb at smoothing things over. Some basic accounting awareness is required in order to keep track of allocating costs to property accounts and handling incoming and outgoing rents. Property managers often have a lettings background but no longer wish to work evenings and weekends. Others may have started out in an administrative role and moved into property management, as it is often slightly better paid.

SALARY: Starting at £18-25K, up to £32k for an experienced property manager

CHAPTER 3

FINDING THE RIGHT EMPLOYER, CORPORATE VS INDEPENDENT AGENCIES

When considering a career in estate agency, it's a good idea to think about whether a corporate or independent agency will best suit your working preferences and career aspirations. Corporate agencies are the largest estate agency groups and possess multiple offices (30-300) across the UK and, in some cases, the globe. The largest groups include Countrywide, which is a FTSE 250-listed company that owns around 50 estate agency chains, including Hamptons, Gascoigne-Pees and John D Wood. Operating under the Countrywide umbrella, each chain retains its own branding and established client base in each area. This creates the interesting scenario whereby in a geographical area with 20 estate agency offices, around half of the different agency brands may ultimately be owned by Countrywide. However, they compete against one another for their market share of the available business in that region. Other large corporate agencies include Spicerhaart and Savills.

The other sector of the market is made up of independent agencies. I include franchised chains such as Winkworth in this sector. These offices take on the group brand and processes of the parent company, however, they are owned and run by private individuals. Independent agencies include those with multiple offices, some with as many as 15 to 20, and may be a veritable force in their marketplace. Alternatively, there may be a single office in a particular area that competes admirably with the larger chain offices, usually as a result of the experience and personality of the owner. Within each residential area there will be an agent who typically sells more houses than flats, an agent who is known to sell the biggest or most expensive properties, and one who has a high turnover of low to mid-range homes in the area. Some agencies will specialise in ex-local authority housing stock, while others may only sell riverfront apartments.

How will the employment experience vary between these two types of agencies?

Regarding recruitment, a corporate agency will usually have a HR department that handles the entire process and may be recruiting for a range of different roles at any given time. Typically, the interview process will be rigorous and will possibly include aptitude and personality tests, group interviews, where candidates engage together and are assessed directly against one another, as well as one-to-one interviews. When you start work with a corporate agency, you'll most likely spend your first week in a group training session alongside other recruits. You'll complete a formulated training process designed to cover business processes, use of the computer system, basic sales skills and a section covering property law. The legal training is largely designed to protect the company from being sued if you breach the law, and puts the onus on the employee to take their legal responsibilities seriously.

After completing this training, your manager or HR officer will set your personal targets and you will commence working in the office. You may only have a limited amount of input regarding which office you are sent to. At regular intervals, your performance will be assessed by either your office manager or HR officer. Any employment issues will often involve a trip to head office. In terms of the day-to-day job experience, the offices will be well presented in accordance with the group branding and will be well equipped with a modern software system that enables communication between offices and allows head office to run activity reports centrally. Centralised teams in head office will tend to take care of specific functions, such as lettings administration and marketing. Your role within the office is likely to be very specific.

Hence your training and direction will be focused towards successfully meeting your sales or lettings targets.

Opportunities for career progression are usually very good, with accelerated training programmes to fast track the most promising employees. There will be a high emphasis on staff retention and progression. On the other hand, there will be limited fluidity with regards to salaries and roles, as these will be structured with grades according to your job title and responsibilities.

An active social side is another great perk of working for a corporate agency, so it usually appeals to those who enjoy mixing with colleagues outside of work. Christmas parties are a big annual event, with large venues hosting the entire group of offices, bringing with it the inevitable chaos this entails! There will typically be an annual awards ceremony for the top performers, with the best 10 to 20 employees being treated to a group holiday or handed keys to a brand new upgraded company vehicle.

So, what are the downsides to working for a corporate agency? You may feel you are just one of many in a massive group of employees and that your personal contribution is either not visible or unrecognised. You may never meet the actual business owner, who is unlikely to know your name, let alone your skills or aspirations. You are unlikely to be able to influence the direction the company takes in terms of marketing, business strategy or how the resources for the offices are allocated. Where you sit and when you get to take your holidays might even be out of your hands, too.

In terms of gaining experience, although the training programmes are likely to be superior to those offered by a smaller business, the experience you'll gain might only be in your allocated role. Therefore, it's unlikely you'll be exposed to other areas of the business and learn about how they operate.

So, how does working for a small independent agency compare?

The independent agencies that have 15 to 20 offices will closely resemble corporate agencies in terms of structure, training and your day-to-day experience, although the business owner or managing director will be more likely to know your name, which office you work in and, crucially, if you are on target or not. So, to give a more precise comparison, we'll assume here that a small, independent agent represents a business with three or fewer offices.

To begin with, the recruitment process will be far more personal. The business owner or office manager will have selected your CV for a specific role. They will usually be present for at least one of the interviews, which are more likely to focus on your skills and experience rather than involve systematic testing. Your contract and the terms of your job offer will be decided by the same parties who interviewed you, and they are likely to be more open to negotiation than a large corporate with set employment grades.

Although you may have some sort of induction training, the majority of your first week will be spent in the office going out on viewings with colleagues and getting to know the vendors and properties. Over a period of six months, you will become integrated into the day-to-day running of the office, getting to know the entire process of your job, whether that is in sales or lettings. If you are in a mixed sales and lettings office, you will absorb some of the processes and knowledge for that part of the business, too, as you will be exposed to the activities and conversations of your colleagues. The training approach is likely to be 'in at the deep end and sink or swim'. You may well meet the business owner during training, or during your first review, and your personal target will be regularly discussed with them or the office manager. This will provide you with a firm sense of your contribution to the business. Having said that, not all of the smaller agencies are run to the same standard. Some will be better organised and have greater leadership and direction than others. Not everyone who opens their own business will make a good manager, organiser or boss. Consequently, with a smaller business, there is a greater risk that you might be entering a workplace mess.

In my experience, if the office is untidy, the existing staff are shabbily dressed or the window display and/or website are out of date, there is a good chance this reflects the state of affairs within the business. If you notice these things at the interview stage, open your eyes to the possibility this may not be the best start to your career. That's not to say that all corporate offices are expertly run and problem-free, but in larger firms there are fixed business standards to be met and a structure in place to monitor them. Your boss will be under pressure to meet performance targets and will be more likely to focus on getting the best from their team, etc., than a one man (or woman) band who may be overwhelmed with the multiple administrative, tax and legal demands involved in running a small business.

In terms of career progression and security, without a doubt the larger companies offer more options for movement between offices, as and when you are ready to progress in your role. They may also have the means to offer you better benefits, with private healthcare and personal pension schemes, etc. With regards to job security, in times of financial difficulty and market fluctuations, the larger chains have bigger financial resources. This doesn't mean your job is any more secure, as, during lean times, they will scrutinise their overheads every bit as much as a smaller firm. If anything, although the smaller firm may be financially more risky, there is perhaps a greater chance of the owner demonstrating loyalty towards a team they know personally than, say, a CEO may show towards a single employee or group of employees amongst several hundred.

CHAPT

INTERVIEWS, SALAF
AND COMMISSIⴑⵏ⸁ⵏ⸁ⵙ⸗

The interview process for estate agency is much the same as in other industries. You may be invited to a telephone interview or an initial face-to-face meeting, which will enable the employer to select perhaps two or three candidates for a second, more thorough interview.

A job offer may be made at a further meeting, proposed by email or arrive via the recruitment company. The offer will usually commence with a base salary, hours, holiday, etc., and set out the commission package and any other benefits.

Interview success, what to expect...

This book does not cover job hunting, CV presentation or interview techniques. For those looking for guidance on these topics, there is already a huge amount of general information available.

an interview for a job with an estate agency basics are as follows:

ar a clean business suit and shirt, with the addition of tie for men. Personal presentation is very important in the industry, and the employer is looking for client facing staff, so shave, get a haircut, polish your shoes and arrive on time.

In certain parts of London, for example, prime central London, or the trendiest parts of north and east London, you may wish to present a little more individuality. For example, if you are a lady going to an interview in Kensington, a decent pair of heels and a high-end branded handbag will be essential (even if it's borrowed). If you can, take a look through the window of the estate agents before your interview and see how the staff are dressed. I once wholly underestimated the quality of dress required for an interview in an upmarket Central London office, and looked positively shabby in comparison to the rest of the highly polished team inside. It wasn't a good start and I consequently wasn't offered the job. For the trendier parts of London, an employer may well appreciate a touch of individual style and personality coming through, as that will also appeal to their clients. If in doubt, stay on the cautious side of formal professional dress, but be aware of the local status quo in terms of workplace attire.

2) Before the interview, make sure you read the company website and the LinkedIn profile of your interviewer. Think about the skills they are likely to be looking for and try to put across what you think you can bring to the team. Don't try to be too clever, and don't take over in the interview. Be positive and express genuine interest in the role, whilst conveying the message you are a hardworking person who is quick to learn. As well as analysing your skillset, your potential employer will be looking to see if your personality will be a good fit in the office, so aim to come across as someone who is going to be easy to work with and manage.

FAQ 3. What questions should I ask in an interview?

Answer: Let your interviewer lead the meeting and, when prompted (usually towards the end of the meeting and if the questions have not already been answered), try to get as clear a picture as possible on the following details; these will be essential to understanding your commission package potential if you receive a job offer:

What is the office/relevant department turnover (the amount of commission brought in by the office) for the last 12 months?

Is that a stable figure or is it unusually high or low? Is the turnover growing?

Does that figure include other income revenues such as

IFA referral income (if it's a sales job) or lettings renewals income (if it's a lettings job)?

On average, what level of commission is earned from new business (the total commission earned from new sales or lettings) each year?

Is the office on target for this year? What is the office/department target?

For that target/turnover, how many negotiators are there on the team?

Ask the above questions and write down the answers – it will be essential for you to have them to hand if you receive a job offer.

It's not nosy or impolite to ask these questions. You need to understand the size of the office turnover so you can get an idea of your earning potential should you receive an offer.

Other useful questions:

Who is the biggest competitor to the agency in the area? (It's a good idea to look at potential competitors' websites in advance so you are familiar with the names). This is a useful question as the competitor could also be a potential employer. It won't hurt to find out how the company you're interviewing with competes against it.

How much will I earn?

As well as the figures set out in Chapter 2, understanding the typical commission structures within the industry is essential in order to accurately predict the income from any position, whether it's Area Manager or Junior Negotiator. This topic will come up during any dealings with recruitment companies or with direct applications. This is because salaries within the estate agency industry vary greatly. Top London agents in senior positions can earn as much as £150,000 per annum. Those running their own successful agencies can earn an equivalent amount, if not more. However, the vast majority of employees within the industry will earn much closer to the national average income, earning between £20,000 to 30,000 per annum, particularly when starting out. The salary figures presented here are correct to 2016, and did not change very much in the preceding decade.

Typical basic salaries for a trainee in sales or lettings based in London and the South East start at £10,000 to 15,000. In other parts of the UK, basic salaries can be anywhere between £8,000 to £10,000 per annum. To properly evaluate any package on offer, it's essential to find out the turnover of the office in the past 12-18 months, and to ascertain how many other negotiators were employed during that time. This is where the answers to your interview questions will really come in handy.

Your final salary is likely to be the make or break of your income for the next couple of years. Consequently, it's essential for you to carefully review the package that you're offered and break it down into its component parts. Taking a job offer without doing the research can penalise you financially for years to come. It's much more difficult to justify a pay rise when the employer knows your weak spots and failings than to negotiate a better starting package when you have delivered the promise of being a top rate employee. Also, bear in mind that some of the turnover figures quoted to you during the interview may have been slightly exaggerated in order to present the company in a better light.

Pooled office commission

The most straightforward package that may be offered to you will be a combination of a basic salary along with a percentage of 'pooled office commission'. To understand how this relates to actual earnings, you need to know the average turnover of the office you will be working in. For instance, if the office generates an average of £50,000 per month in sales commission and you will earn 2% of the office commission, your basic salary of £15,000 will be topped up with a further £12,000, meaning that an average annual salary of £27,000 will be earned.

The major advantage of pooled commission is that

assuming the office is well established, your earnings are likely to be more stable than with other commission packages, and you will receive a more consistent salary from day one. As you progress in your career, your commission percentage may increase so that a senior negotiator may earn 3% of the monthly office income, a sales manager 4% and a director 5%. Basic salaries may also increase with promotion. Due to the nature of the property market and irrespective of your commission package, your salary will vary depending on market conditions and the time of year. Typically, busy periods are February to June and September to November, with less business being transacted during the rest of the year. Other parts of the UK vary. Many find the summer months are the busiest, with 60% to 70% of transactions occurring between May and September. Bearing in mind these fluctuations, even on a pooled commission structure and in a top performing sales office, your January pay packet may be as much as 25% less than in July.

The office is likely to be staffed by a team of two to three negotiators and a valuations or branch manager, who will gain new instructions and manage the running of the office and staff. If all staff in the office are working towards a common goal, i.e. as many sales agreed as possible, your working environment will likely comprise team-based activities, where you support each other's deals, cover each other's viewings and theoretically agree more sales than if you were working towards individual commission targets. As within many sales industries, one month can vary greatly from another. By pooling your team's efforts, the impact of irregularities in personal performance or the disaster of a lost sale or letting (known as a fall through) can be lessened by the backup of your teammates' successes each month. On the flip side, of course, is that if your colleagues are off sick, have a bad run, or are just plain lazy/useless, then your hard work and efforts can be wiped out, as a poor overall office performance waters down your share. In my opinion, the pooled commission structure works well when the office is staffed by a more mature and experienced team, rather than one made up of fresh-to-the-industry workers who are still learning their trade.

Individual commission packages at the manager's discretion

Many of the most established chains of estate agents prefer to offer individual commission, but at the manager's discretion. This means that your basic salary may be higher, as much as £30,000 per annum compared to £10,000 to 15,000 in the same area. However, your commission is paid quarterly and is undisclosed to your team members. The main advantage of this type of structure is that your basic salary may be enough to ensure that your essential monthly outgoings are covered every single month, unlike a pooled or individual commission structure. The office manager is able to reward hard work, performance and overall contribution to the office at their discretion and not just base it on actual sales figures. If you are systematically a hard worker and ultimately a good agent, your manager may overlook short-term fluctuations and pay a commission based on a longer term, bigger picture view of your performance.

The downside of this type of commission package is that in a small team setting, you are relying on a good relationship with your manager and a more subjective opinion of your performance.

In these types of companies, there may be a split in the type of properties you are engaged in, i.e. flats, mid-range houses or top-end properties. This is to the benefit of the office, as you'll become the expert in your field. At the same time, if the house market slows down while your flat department is still going strong, you may feel the impact of the failings of others, while not necessarily being rewarded when they do well in the future. Despite these drawbacks, companies operating under this arrangement tend to have much higher staff retention rates, with employees staying five to 10 years rather than the average two to three year stint.

Individual commission packages

The chart below shows the typical percentage of commission paid to a negotiator on an individual commission package, and how this increases as they reach certain fee incomes. Typically, the commission year runs from January to December.

Fee income generated	Commission share paid to negotiator
First £49,999	8%
£50,000-99,999	10%
£100,000-£149,999	12%
£150,000 and over	15%

By far, the most common commission structure will involve a basic salary plus a percentage of all sales either exchanged or completed over the previous month. Often, this is set on a sliding scale, with increasing percentages paid as annual targets are met. For example, the first £50,000 of fees achieved is paid at 8%, the next £25,000 at 10%, with any deals over £75,000 being paid at 12% and deals over £100,000 at 15%. The benefit to the employer is that these targets are set so that for 75% of the year, the majority of the commission paid will be at 8% to 10%. 'Average' performing negotiators will only ever achieve this level of pay. The benefit to the best performing negotiators is that their success is directly rewarded by their pay and the best negotiators enjoy a high rate of pay in the latter part of the year, with the commission payable from January to December. This means that a quiet December may be buffeted by a higher commission rate. On the downside, dropping back down to a lower rate of commission with each new year can be very demotivating for many negotiators.

A new employee is unlikely to reach the higher commission rates in the first year, as these usually require a pipeline of sales agreed from the previous year, i.e. sales which are agreed in October to December, which consequently reach exchange and completion in January to February. A cold start with no pipeline to carry you into the year will prevent all but the top performing agents achieving the higher rates of commission. On these packages, the commission structure is often maintained after progression to senior negotiator or sales manager, with an additional percentage of the total office commission also being paid.

Individual commission packages mean an individual's salary is down to them. It rewards the most talented and hardest-working agents. The very nature of this payment method creates an entirely more competitive working environment in the office. For the clients, this may result in a higher sales price, as negotiators pit their buyers against one another to ensure theirs is the one to do the deal. It may also mean that your colleagues become your enemies, with each negotiator bending the office rules. For example, in the majority of offices the negotiator will 'own' the 'applicant' (buyer). When a new instruction comes to the office, each negotiator may be given seven days to show the new property to their applicants, after which time any negotiator in the office can introduce the property to any buyer. In real terms, if you have two weeks off, you may return to find that your best five buyers, who you have been assisting for several weeks or months, are now buying properties with your colleagues. Despite the time and energy you have put in with them in the past, you will not be earning anything from their purchase. Ultimately, the reverse is true when your colleagues go on holiday, as you may also be able to sell to their buyers. Individual commission packages are therefore destined to create a highly competitive working environment.

Fee income from other sources

When presented with a commission package at the job offer stage, other likely elements of the offer may include referral fees. These can be earned by selling your applicants additional services, often in the form of financial services leads. Most estate agents will partner up with a financial services firm and book appointments for their applicants to speak to their in-house mortgage broker. Most negotiators will be set a referral target per week and bonuses may be paid as part of their monthly salaries. Similarly, many agents have a recommended surveyor who they refer business to. Typically, this type of bonus will equate to £25 to £50 per successful referral, i.e. the agent refers the business and the applicant signs up for the service. Realistically, this income stream will only account for 5% of the overall income for most negotiators, but the employer often uses it to bulk up the appearance of an otherwise minimal basic salary package.

The other major element to query when assessing a salary package is when the commission is actually payable to you and when it can be 'clawed back'.

On the sales side, the majority of companies will pay your commission share once the property has completed. Some will pay the individual commission share once the property has exchanged, which may mean you receive your commission share four to six weeks earlier on average than if it is paid on completion. If your employer pays commission on completion, it's useful to know whether they require the payment from the vendor to be cleared first, or whether they will pay you in good faith. The finer detail of your contract can mean the difference between hanging on for months waiting for a big commission payment or getting paid promptly by your employer once your job is done, i.e. at the exchange of contracts.

On the lettings side, the details to note are as follows: if a tenant moves into a property on a 12-month tenancy, but after six months give two months' notice and leaves, how will the commission payment be handled? In most cases, the lettings negotiator who agreed the transaction would be paid the full commission for the 12-month let when the tenant moved. If the tenant leaves before the end of the year, the negotiator would then have to reimburse any months where they had not rented the property. This reflects the typical situation for the agency, which will also repay a percentage of the commission back to the landlord. This situation is commonly referred to as 'clawback'. Other agencies may prefer to pay on a monthly cumulative basis, which removes this issue. However, this means the negotiator's earnings will be very low for the first three to six months of their employment, whilst they build up their base of lettings deals. The structure of lettings commission will be determined by the charging system in place at the agency.

This leads onto the question of a 'guarantee period'.

Whether you are in a sales or a lettings position, there will be a period when you need to establish a pipeline of agreed sales or lets before you start to see your commission filtering through. As part of your package offer, you will almost certainly be given a three-month guarantee period. This means your basic salary will be topped up whilst you build your pipeline. You need to read the small print in your contract concerning guarantees, because if you leave the company during your guarantee period or are asked to leave, you may be required to repay any additional sums received above your basic salary. Guarantees are usually paid at 60% to 70% of your basic salary. For example, if your basic salary is £15,000, your likely guarantee for the first three months will equate to three months' pay at the pro rata rate of £25,000.

Another element to consider with regards to lettings and salary packages is whether you will receive a payment based on 'renewals'. A 'renewal' is when a tenancy you agreed 12 months ago (or six months ago if you agreed a six month contract) reaches the end of its term and is renewed for a further one. Some agencies will pay the lettings negotiator a commission when the tenancy is renewed, often requiring them to handle the negotiation of the rent, the terms of the renewal and the paperwork. In other firms, this will be handled by the admin team, with no payment for the negotiator who agreed the original letting. Other income sources in the lettings environment can be earned by selling insurance products to landlords and tenants, such as rent guarantee insurance or contents insurance. Some firms will also pay a commission if the negotiator sells a particular furnishing package or inventory service.

In a sales negotiator package, further income often comes in the form of recommending a particular IFA or surveyor, and there is often a panel of solicitors who will pay a referral commission if the buyer or vendor uses them.

Car and benefits

The final part of the package will relate to your car. Some employers will offer to provide you with a company vehicle, while others will pay you an allowance towards running costs. At first sight, a company car might seem a very attractive proposition. Be warned, though, you may be restricted to using it for work only, and you will take on a substantial additional tax burden with respect to the vehicle, which will be considered as a 'benefit in kind'. In addition, vandals often target branded cars and should an accident occur whilst it is parked, there is less likelihood of the other party leaving a number. This is because people assume the company will cover the cost of repairs. In reality, the employee will be held responsible for any damage and made to pay for it up to an excess limit. In terms of maintenance, the car will usually be booked in for an annual service and any damage will be repaired automatically, with the cost being deducted from the employee's following month's salary. This is designed to ensure staff members treat their company car with respect. However, it can mean repair costs for minor scratches are deducted from their earnings. Full details of the car agreement should be provided with your contract.

A pooled car scheme is often a better option, with no additional tax payable and damages only charged to you if you were actually at fault. A car allowance can work well and is usually paid as an additional monthly amount. Most companies will require your vehicle to be no more than two years old and in good order. It's worth bearing in mind that frequent viewings and short trips will add additional wear and tear on the car, and you will need to upgrade your insurance to cover you for business use.

Further allowances for petrol and mobile phone use can look inviting, but these are frequently accompanied by hefty paperwork and, in many cases, the time required to complete this work renders claiming your allowance an unattractive proposition.

Working hours

Working hours can range from the extreme to the more realistic. When starting out, you may be required to work from 8am to 8pm Monday to Friday and every Saturday (and even some Sundays). With time and experience, better working hours can often be negotiated, with a typical agent working from 9am to 6.30pm Monday to Friday and every other Saturday, often with a weekday given in lieu of weekends worked.

Working hours also vary greatly from one firm to another. If you have young children or regular sporting commitments, the hours may simply be unrealistic as a long-term career choice. However, the first two to three years in the industry will often require more hours per week, and these will lessen once you have progressed in your career. Long hours and weekend work are one of the major reasons why people leave the industry, so be honest with yourself at the start if you know this will be a compromise too far. Even if a company only requires you to work until 5.30pm or 6pm, the reality is that most applicants will need to view properties outside of their own working hours, so you will need to facilitate this by extending your own working day. In terms of the working time directive, you will be required to 'voluntarily' sign away your rights to working a maximum 48-hour week.

Annual leave usually equates to 20 days per annum,

with at least three to four of those deducted to cover Christmas closures. Therefore, you can expect to have three full weeks holiday per year, give or take a few days. Bank holidays are viewed as normal working days in around 50% of agencies. Maternity and sick pay are likely to equate to a statutory payment based on your basic salary only. This is particularly important if you are considering starting a family. After several years of working for a company, your salary, for example, could be £25,000+ per annum of commission, with a basic rate of £15,000. Your maternity pay is likely to be based only on your basic salary, which would represent a massive drop in income during your maternity leave. Paternity allowances will have less of an impact, as the time away from work is much reduced. Again, reading your contract thoroughly will ensure you don't get any nasty surprises.

The average new negotiator won't be offered a pension scheme or healthcare benefits. These are only likely to kick in at Branch Manager or Area Manager level.

Your contract may well include a clause preventing you from working for a competing agency after you leave. Before committing to a new contract, you should carefully consider the impact of this clause on your future career plans.

CHAPTER 5

YOUR FIRST WEEK IN THE JOB:
THE BASICS

What can you expect in your first few days as an estate agent? As I touched on earlier, your experience will vary based on the type of agency you join. With a corporate agency, you will undoubtedly go through an induction programme, which may take a week to 10 days to complete and will include tests and group sessions to ensure you are ready to hit the floor running. These may be interspersed with sessions in the office to give you a mix of both. You'll also spend a bit of time covering basic HR and IT issues, along with sorting out your car and any parking permits.

As a junior negotiator in a small agency, you're most likely to be invited to shadow a colleague for a few days to get you started. They will show you the basics of the computer system and get you out and about with them on viewings. They may be largely disinterested in helping you out, or simply too busy, so you will have to show initiative to get on with what you need to do. At a point early on you will be handed a list of available properties and expected to quickly absorb a whole host of relevant facts about them, including their location, whether they are owner-occupied or tenanted and how to get access to them, i.e. are there keys in the office? You'll also need to memorise how much notice the vendors need for a viewing, if they have pets, if there is an alarm, if their property has been available for a while, if it has just had a price reduction, if it is in good order, and if there are damp issues or a short lease...the list goes on.

For lettings, you need to know two very fundamental things: whether the property is furnished and what date it is available from.

The volume of information thrown at you can be quite overwhelming, so stay calm, print off a list of available properties, go through them with your colleague and ask lots of questions while putting yourself in the shoes of a potential tenant or buyer. Listen carefully to the answers and write them down next to the relevant properties on your list. You are going to need the information whilst you find your feet. After a few weeks, the information on each property will mostly be in your head, or you will know enough about the computer system to be able to find everything out for yourself. In the meantime, keep the property list to hand at all times, as there won't always be someone there to ask for help. It can be awkward to be on your own at a viewing with no information whilst your applicant fires questions at you.

Useful jargon for your first week

You will see the following shorthand terms used extensively in diaries and applicant registrations notes:

MAP - Meet at the property

MIO - Meet in the office

FTB - First time buyer

BTL – Buy-to-let investor

V - Vendor

LL - Landlord

NS - No show, person booked viewing but didn't show or cancelled at the last minute

CXL - Cancelled viewing

HOT – A motivated applicant

PRED - Price reduction

NEG - Negotiator

PW - Per week

PCM - Per calendar month

General terms used in day-to-day working:

Applicant - A buyer or tenant. Each negotiator will have a list of applicants registered under their name to keep in contact with regarding properties to buy or rent.

Waster - Someone who is known to waste your time. They might like booking viewings but either won't make an offer or will make ones that are too low. They may also have unrealistic expectations for their budget or simply won't show up to appointments or provide feedback. Sometimes applicants are unfairly labelled; one person's waster can be another's hot buyer/tenant, if they know how to work with them. There is some trial and error involved in learning to distinguish between a motivated applicant and a time waster.

Downsizer - Someone who is selling up to move into a smaller home. They may be an older person, a couple releasing equity, or a divorcee.

Developer – This is a general term and refers to a wide range of professional investors. At the lower end of the scale, it might be used to describe private buyers who are looking for properties to add value to by refurbishing, extending or splitting into flats. Usually, the agency will encourage the developer to use them to sell the properties on once they're finished. Although there is rarely a written agreement, agents will quickly move on to a more cooperative developer for their most profitable instructions if the working relationship isn't respected.

The basics

Registering applicants

One of the first activities you will be engaged in is registering someone looking to buy or rent. They may walk into the office or make phone contact. You should immediately grab your property list with all your notes and start asking them questions and building a rapport. They may enquire about a specific property or they may just want to find out what you have available. You might start by taking a few bits of information to get you warmed up, or you may prefer just to chat with them generally about what they are looking for. A typical conversation will go along the lines of:

Applicant – "I have seen a property for sale/let on XYZ road, can I arrange a viewing?"

Neg – "Yes, no problem. What's that one priced at, please? (This question is used as a shortcut to find the property on the list, which is likely to be in price order. It reduces the risk of any confusion over which property they are interested in.)

Applicant - "It's on your website at £300pw/£300,000."

Neg – "Oh, yes, it's on so and so street. Yes, Ok, perhaps I can take a few details and we can get you booked in." (Remember to take their name, telephone number and email address, etc., sometimes even their home address.)

The WRONG next question from the neg is – "Ok, when do you want to see it?"

You first need to qualify when the person wishes to move, why they are looking to move, where they are looking to move to, and why that property is of interest to them. You also need to establish their budget. In short:

WHEN

WHY

WHERE

WHAT

And then finally...

THEIR BUDGET

"Why go through all that?" I hear you ask. Surely the applicant knows what they are looking for? Well, you need to understand the motivation and needs of the applicant before you commit to show them a property. Failure to properly talk through the above questions will mean wasted time for both parties in terms of inappropriate viewings.

So, let us briefly break these questions down further.

When are you looking to move?

Lettings applicants will often have a date range in mind connected with a new job or the end of their current tenancy. Sales applicants may say, "When we find the right thing." Your next question should therefore be, "What have you seen so far?" If the applicant has been looking for six months or more, unless they have a genuine reason why they haven't bought or rented, you can be confident this isn't a HOT applicant. You may still decide to take them out on viewings, but just don't invest too much time on them.

If they are looking to buy and have just started looking, one to two weeks is a good time to start working with them, and this can stretch up to two months. Ask them if they found anything they liked, and talk through their preferences.

Why are you looking to move?
You might hear responses such as, "Our landlord is selling our flat."/ "We need another bedroom because I'm pregnant."/ "We are moving closer to friends, work, etc." These are all highly informative answers that will help you identify the right sort of properties for your applicant.

Where are you looking?
Enquiring, "Which areas are you considering?" will help you understand if the applicant is looking in a few specific roads or several counties. The latter response indicates that your chance of being the agent who sells or lets them a property is quite limited. A truly hot applicant will be

specific in where they want to be, having researched the areas and narrowed them down.

What are you looking to buy?

In response to this question, you may get a list of requirements as long as your arm, or simply a response such as, "a two-bed flat". You will need to identify their actual needs rather than their preferences, i.e. they want something in good order, but are willing to decorate if needed. They want two bedrooms but the second could be smaller as it will only be used as a study. Try to take on board any non-negotiable needs, such as, "The property must be within x distance of a particular station or school," and let some of the others sit more loosely in your mind. Applicants rarely end up with a perfect property that meets their needs 100%, and their priorities may change as the viewings progress. For example, they may start looking for a garden flat but end up renting a larger property without outside space once they have seen how small the gardens are for their budget. Or they may request a house with a south facing garden, but in the end buy one with a north facing one because they like the house enough to make that compromise.

What is your budget?

This can be both a pleasant surprise and a moment of

quiet disbelief! Applicants that have already done their homework will know roughly what they can get in their chosen area and will have a set of expectations to match their budget. Others will need some guidance. If their budget doesn't match their expectations for properties in the areas you cover, you will either need to help them revise their expectations or suggest some other, more affordable areas. It doesn't matter where we are in the UK, we all aspire to buy or rent something better than we can afford. The viewing process often shines a bright light on the reality of the budget vs expectations.

<u>If you are helping a sales applicant, the key question to finish off the conversation is: How are you intending to finance your purchase?</u>

This is a nice, open question, which will quickly reveal quite a lot about your buyer. They may have a deposit in place and a mortgage agreed or they may need to sell their property (in which case you need to find out if it is in an area covered by your company, as it could be a potential valuation opportunity). If they have a property to sell, ask if it is on the market and if they have had any interest. If it isn't on the market as yet, have they had it valued? This will identify how far along they are in the moving process and, crucially, how much time and energy you should spend on them. If someone is a 'potential vendor' then you will need to spend more time nurturing the relationship in order to try and get their property on the market.

<u>If you are helping a lettings applicant, you will need to ask them about their income and financial stability. This will help you to determine their ability to pay the rent.</u>

Explain that you need to ask a few questions about their income and employment status, as there will be a referencing process to complete if they see a property they like. Typically, they will need to be earning at least 30 times the monthly rent. For example, if the rent is £1000 per month, they would need a sole or joint income of £30,000 per year from a permanent job in order for the monthly rental amount to be considered 'affordable'. This calculation assumes that after paying income tax, their monthly take home pay would be sufficient to cover the rent and bills and leave some leftover to live on. Different agencies employ different calculations, but the end result will be similar. Potential tenants must also pass a referencing process, which will include a credit check, employment reference and a current landlord reference, if applicable. Students will typically require a guarantee from a parent, who in turn will need to meet the referencing criteria. Self-employed applicants will need to provide their previous year's tax return as proof of earnings.

Alternatively, if tenants can't meet the referencing criteria, they may be able to pay several months' rent in advance. Before you book a viewing with a lettings applicant, you should be confident they will meet the referencing requirements - otherwise you are wasting your time.

Once you have completed the process of qualifying the applicant, you can then review your list of available properties, talking them through the positives and negatives of each one and getting feedback. In the end you will hopefully have one to three good options to show them.

In a busy market, you won't have time to help every applicant that contacts the office, so you need to learn to identify those who are most likely to buy or rent in the immediate future. When the market is quieter, you will have more time to spend with individual applicants. It's easy to feel obligated to try and help everyone who comes into the office, and it's certainly the case that you should treat all applicants with courtesy. However, you are ultimately being paid by your vendor or landlord to sell or let their property, so you are not obliged to arrange a viewing simply because an applicant demands it. Your job is to agree the maximum possible number of deals, and in order to be effective at this you should only arrange viewings with buyers and tenants that you have properly qualified. You need to be confident they are motivated and are able to proceed with a purchase or rental.

Booking a viewing

When you have successfully matched an applicant with some suitable properties, "When do you wish to view?" will be the next natural question.

I have two pointers here. First, it's useful to know if the property is empty or occupied. If the latter is the case then the occupants will no doubt need to be informed about the viewing. If they are tenants, they will need at least 24-hours' notice. Find out if the office holds keys to the property and what the code is for them (most agencies have a system of keyrings with codes, so if you drop the keys in the street by accident, the address won't be revealed). You'll also need to know if there are any special requirements for accessing the property, such as an alarm code, pets in the property or a concierge that needs informing of the visit in advance.

Planning your viewings

When you are booking in your viewings, you might also like to consider adding a property that may fit the applicant's requirements, even if it is marginally above their budget or outside of their initial search criteria. Adding on one more visit at the end of two or three viewings won't be too difficult if it's already organised and you have the keys with you. If during the viewings you find it's not worth adding it on, for example, you've established they won't like something about that property, or they are clearly just looking around and not ready to commit to making an offer, you can always scrap it, but it's nice to have a wild card to hand. In general, it's human nature to want more than we can afford. With that in mind, you have a better chance of someone making an offer if you show them a property at the top or just beyond their top-end budget. This will probably be the best property they have seen, and hence they are more likely to make an offer on it than the one you show them that is under their maximum budget, which will undoubtedly involve more compromises. That's not to say people always spend the maximum they can, but showing the applicant what the extra money will buy can be a useful tool in helping them understand pricing in the marketplace and what their budget will deliver. If you don't try to offer them a more expensive option, you may find the applicant leaves your viewing tour with the impression that what they really want to buy or rent isn't available to them, when really if they increased their budget by 5% to 10% they would probably find their ideal property. Their expectations have simply exceeded the money they have decided to spend or can spend. Many people reading this may think, *"That is such a typical estate agent attitude. What makes them think they know better than me concerning what I want to buy or how much I want to spend?"* What I am not talking about here is hard selling your applicant into buying or renting something they can't afford. Your goal is to expose them to the correct range of properties so they can gain a better understanding of why some properties command a higher price than others. This means they will view what is for sale in their budget with an educated level of price awareness. In the long run, it will make it easier for them to decide what is right for them. Perhaps they would rather have a smaller or shabbier property in their ideal location than something that is newly renovated but will mean a longer commute to work.

Most properties are priced with location, size, condition and features in mind, so if you see three properties and they all offer the characteristics you have asked for, but they are not close enough to your workplace, you would appreciate it if the agent brought along an extra set of keys for a place that is not quite what you asked for but offers an easier commute.

If you have seen three, one-bedroom garden flats, and found all were dark and pokey inside, and the agent brought along keys for a first floor, two-bed flat that was affordable, light and spacious, you would reconsider whether you were willing to sacrifice living space for garden space. Even if you didn't end up buying or renting that property, it would have helped you to prioritise your criteria.

Keys & details

Before you leave the office, plan where you are going to go and in which order. This is especially important if the area is unfamiliar to you. Think about where you will park and keep the office telephone number and your mobile phone to hand. Also, give yourself some time before your appointment to get the keys organised. Note the important elements of the property and print off some details. As you progress in your role, you'll streamline this process and you will know the details of each property by heart and be able to organise viewings effortlessly. However, to begin with, there is a steep learning curve. Once you have visited 50% to 60% of the properties on the agency's books, your stress levels will subside, as you will know at least some of what you are going to see in advance. To begin with, you'll find it reassuring to have the property details to hand. Some agents believe that offering the applicant a set of printed details will make them more likely to consider that property. In my opinion, if somebody likes a property they will buy or rent it irrespective of the property details, which should be used more as a tool for marketing the property and booking in viewings. When you are starting out with your viewings, taking the details with you will feel like a bit of a safety blanket.

Going on a viewing

In your first week, it's a good idea to tag along on a few of your colleague's viewings so that you get a feel for the process. Generally, you'll meet your applicant in the office or at one of the properties. Many agents prefer to get the client to come to the office. This means reduced time waiting outside a property and, more importantly, it gives you the opportunity to talk to the applicant en route about themselves. You can ask then what they do for a living, find out their family situation and get a feel for how well they know the area, etc. Being face-to-face with an applicant means you can usually glean a lot more information than you can if you speak to them over the phone. This is where your people skills come into play. You need to make them feel welcome and put them at ease, as well as getting them excited about viewing the properties.

Handling the keys and opening doors

When you arrive at the property, you should have the keys to hand. Once inside, you should always keep them in your hand and never walk out of the front door without first checking that you have them. The stress and anticipation of your first few viewings will do all sorts of strange things to the keys. On numerous occasions, I have experienced negotiators returning to the office stressed and huffing about not having the right keys, or the keys not working, when in fact they had the correct set all along. It's amazing what your mind can do to a set of keys. When you are very stressed it's possible to trick yourself into believing they don't work. If you have properly prepared for the viewing you'll know the address, so before you put the key in to try it, check you are at the right door and that the key code matches the property you are trying to access. If you have three sets of keys with you, check that you have the right set. Then calmly try to open the door. This may sound utterly obvious and ridiculous, but when you are standing on a doorstep with your applicant waiting behind you (and sometimes their entire extended family) there is enormous potential for stress and embarrassment when you cannot get inside the property.

Showing the property

Everyone develops their own style of showing a property, but there are some basics that will help you get the most out of the viewing. In an ideal world, you will have visited the property in advance, put on the lights and ensured the presentation is spot on. In reality, most viewing schedules will not allow for this luxury.

As you enter the property, as quickly as possible, turn on any lights and draw back any curtains or shutters. Start with the main living area and kitchen and follow with any outside space. Then move onto bedrooms and bathrooms. You can point out any positive features as you show each room, but do not talk incessantly; allow the applicant a little headspace to digest what they are seeing.

As you progress around the property, try to walk a little way ahead of your applicants so you can switch on lights and discretely hide any personal items, such as underwear left on the floor, before they are seen. However, stay out of the room as your applicant looks around it, this way it will feel bigger and allow them to get a sense of the space rather than looking at you. This is particularly important for bathrooms and smaller spaces. Depending on your applicant's reaction to the property, you may wish to show loft spaces and outbuildings, but don't waste your time doing this if they are really not interested. If the owner is going to be at home, it's a good idea to suggest they step out into the garden or stay in one room and allow you to show the property unaccompanied. Whilst it's handy to have the owner present to answer any questions, most buyers prefer to see the property while they're absent. This way they are free to share their real likes and concerns. Typically, the applicant will be polite and tell the owner they really like the property, only voicing their true opinion, which might not be so positive, once they are outside. When you have finished showing the house, ensure you return to each room to switch off any lights. Also ensure that doors and windows are closed and lock up securely. If in doubt, leave things as you found them.

Asking for an offer

Negotiation skills are a huge topic, which I'll touch on briefly in the next chapter. The one thing you must do in your first week of viewings is ask for an offer. If you don't then quite simply you are not a sales person - you are simply an appointment booking door opener. My first boss used to scream at us as we went out on our viewings, "Don't come back to the office without an offer!" It worked. We made sure we asked for one on every viewing.

So, you have registered the applicant, booked the viewing and now they are stood in the property and they hate it. What do you do? Get them out of there and into another property without delay. Don't let them wander around aimlessly nitpicking.

On occasion, if your applicant is fussing around being negative about a property and you say firmly, but politely, "Ok, if it's not for you then let's go," they may surprise you by saying they actually quite like it. Then you can start the process of dealing with their concerns and discussing an offer that would work for them. Or they may agree to leave straightaway. In that case, you have just saved everyone a lot of time.

The other option is that the applicant may be making positive comments or just being quite quiet and looking around, but you can tell they are thinking it through. When they have had a chance to look around and digest the property, and you have run through their questions, you should ask for an offer. Simply ask, "How much would you be willing to offer for this property?" (Note this is different to asking them if they would like to make an offer.) You may get a definitive response but you are more likely to hear them say, "I would like to think about it," "I am not sure if it's for me," or "I have other things to see." You can then respond with a range of open-ended questions that will help the applicant conclude what it is about the property that is right or wrong. For example, it's Ok if they have other things to see, but how does the property compare in terms of price to other ones they have visited? Suggest a lower price for the property and find out whether that would make it a more tempting prospect. Ask them if the property is better or worse than the last one they saw and find out why. Ask them how that reflects the price they would be willing to pay. By constantly returning to price, you are helping them to focus their mind on what they would be willing to pay and also decide what really matters to them. Most people appreciate there will always be some compromises. If you ask them for an offer they will start to consider whether the property would work for them for the right price. Or they may conclude they would be willing to spend more money to get a better property. This process of asking for an offer needs to be part of every viewing. You may undertake ten viewings and not get a concrete offer, but you will return to the office with a huge amount of information on what will and won't work for the applicant, as well as useful feedback that can help the property owner understand how their property compares to others, and why they may not be receiving offers.

In short, getting into the habit of asking for an offer on every viewing will increase your chances of succeeding in the industry.

FAQ. 4 Is it safe to be alone on viewings, particularly for females?

In 1986, Suzy Lamplugh, a 25-year-old negotiator, disappeared whilst out on a viewing. She was never found, although she was presumed murdered by the man she had met to show a property to. The Suzy Lamplugh Trust was set up to educate those working in the profession, as well as the general public, about personal safety. There are several steps you can take in your job that will improve yours. Your company may have its own personal safety protocol, but either way the following suggestions apply equally to male and female negotiators.

Firstly, you should never leave the office and go out on a viewing without recording in the office diary where you are going, the order of visits and the name, telephone numbers (ideally a work and a mobile one), email address and full home address of the person you are viewing the property with. By following these measures, your colleagues will have a good idea of where you are, and the identity of the viewer.

Trust your instincts. If you speak to someone over the phone or meet someone in the office and their behaviour sparks concern in your mind, don't do the viewing alone. It's not worth the risk. Ask a colleague to accompany you and don't feel embarrassed to flag up your concerns. If someone is being overtly flirtatious and it's making you feel uncomfortable, don't go on the viewing alone. There are people out there who fantasise about having sexual relations with an estate agent. I had an awful experience while out on a viewing when the well-spoken, nicely dressed 'gentleman' decided to take his chance and lunge for a kiss. I was furious and he quickly backed down. It was the last viewing on a Friday night and at the end of it he asked to quickly revisit an empty flat (where he knew we would be alone). In hindsight, I realised his actions were calculated. I have also heard from male colleagues who have had unsettling experiences with both men and women. Therefore, it's important that everyone in the office maintains an awareness of their colleagues' whereabouts. There should also be a distress code agreed within the office. If you are on a viewing and you need help, you should have a discreet code that you can announce to a colleague back in the office. This can be along the lines of, "Please can you tell Frederick (or a similar unusual fake name) that I am late for my next appointment. I am currently at XYZ address with..." (Give your precise location and the name of the person you are with.) Your colleagues should instantly recognise the signal, call the police and come and find you as soon as possible. Usually, the distress code is displayed on a poster in the back office to remind everyone of what to do if a colleague says this phrase. If your viewings are over-running, you should contact the office and, at the end of each day, the office manager should contact each team member to ensure they have safety concluded their viewings (negotiators will often go straight home from their final one). Driving the applicant in your own car rather than agreeing to go in their vehicle is a safer option, too.

If you are intimidated or even attacked on a viewing, you should make as much noise as possible and try to turn your fright into fight. If you have the property keys in your hand, they can be used as a weapon. Try to ensure that you let the person go down the stairs in front of you to prevent being pushed from behind, but ultimately do whatever you can to get out of the property and seek help.

Aside from the possibility of a physical assault, showing someone around a property can present an opportunity for theft. For that reason, it's always a good idea to keep them in view rather than leaving them to wander around alone. Also ask the vendor to remove any small valuables from display, such as cameras and jewellery, etc. These are very easy to sneak into a pocket or bag. I have also had first-hand experience of this and had to deal with a small camera going missing from a flat. The following day, the police discovered that the 'applicant' had visited properties with several agents along the same road, and all the owners had lost an item. He had registered with false details, was smartly dressed (with a leather briefcase) and had a coherent reason for wanting to visit the properties.

The other risk you face as a negotiator is being locked in or out of a property. I know an inventory clerk who got locked in a cellar on a Friday afternoon and wasn't noticed as missing until Monday morning. I personally got locked in a bathroom in the middle of a large new build development where all the flats were empty and my mobile phone was in the kitchen. I have also been locked out on a roof terrace after a door slammed behind me. Luckily, I had my phone and called a colleague who was able to come to the rescue. Accidents happen and when they do you will be very pleased that you properly recorded the viewing in the office diary.

CHAPTER 6

YOUR FIRST YEAR IN THE JOB: DEVELOPING YOUR SKILLSET

Your employment contract is likely to have a probationary period of three to six months. During this time, your employer can give you minimal notice to leave, normally a week. A good employer or manager will sit down with you at the end of your first week to review your performance, highlight any concerns and set out their expectations for the coming two to three weeks. Others will leave you to get on with the job for the first six weeks or so, and then set you some targets to be reviewed around the three-month mark. It all depends on the management and HR structure of the business. The larger the agency, the more structured the review process is likely to be. If you don't have a review meeting in the first two months, it's a good idea to ask for one. That way you are giving the employer the chance to brief you on their expectations. By that point you will have mastered the basics. It's also a good time to ask for extra training on any areas that you are less confident about. Often, this will be in relation to gaining confidence in your negotiation skills or progressing further on sales or lettings.

Developing your skillset

Acquiring basic negotiation skills

Expert negotiation is quite simply an art form. It's all about encouraging people to ask for exactly what they want, whilst working gently around the topic with some increasingly tightening boundaries, so that both parties reach a deal that is not too uncomfortable or too far from their initial expectations. As their career in property progresses, many agents find the negotiation process the most stimulating and exciting part of the job. When negotiations go sour, it can also be very unpleasant for all involved.

Assuming that you have no professional negotiation experience, here is a simple strategy to get you up and running. In this example, we are talking about a sales offer, but the same principles apply to lettings.

Your buyer has a figure they would like to put forward to the vendor, so ask them to justify that offer. In other words, ask them to tell you why they have decided upon that figure. They may tell you they wish to make the offer at less than the asking price because, for example, there is no bath in the property and they really wanted a tub. However, in all other respects, the property could work for them.

You will now contact your vendor and set the offer out for them in the following format.

Firstly, tell them three positive features about the offer. For example:

1. The offer is from a first time buyer couple. They have nothing to sell/no chain, hence they are ideal buyers.

2. The buyers wish to move in by August, which is perfect for you because you need to move before the start of the next school year.

3. The buyers have a mortgage agreed in principle and they have already instructed a solicitor to help them proceed with the purchase.

Now tell them the offer.

At this point, STOP TALKING.

If you don't observe the STOP TALKING rule, you could well find yourself trying to fill the gap in the conversation by suggesting reasons why they might prefer not to take the offer. You will not know what the vendor thinks unless you let them speak.

Give the client a moment or two to breathe and

digest the offer a little bit. They will normally say, "Ok, let me think about it," or they may straightaway say the offer is less than they wanted and they need to mull it over, talk it over with their partner, etc. Either way, stay quiet and calm and just listen to what they have to say. They may ask your opinion on it, which you can give honestly. If you really think you can get them more money, then you must tell them. You can also talk about some of the negative points of the property, such as the lack of a bath. You should explain that the buyers are looking at other properties as well, and point out the risk involved in saying no to the offer, i.e. highlight to them that any offer is a relatively transient thing. Help them to understand the current market conditions and what else has sold and at what price. Don't put pressure on the owner. This will simply make them feel like those boundaries are contracting much too quickly. Time and patience is key. If they outright reject the offer in the first conversation, encourage them to sleep on it and consider what they *would* be willing to take. You need to give the owner time to digest it and start to mentally 'spend the money'. If the offer is really very low and bordering on offensive, and the owner is clearly rattled by the conversation, simply let them know that you are required by law to present all offers you receive and that you will continue to work for them to get the best price you can. Any offer, however low, will ultimately help the owner reflect on their real financial position, and if you receive a better offer next week it will be seen in a more positive light than it would if you hadn't presented the lower offer to them.

When the owner has made their decision and has come back to you, assuming that the answer is no, then you will return to the applicant with a similar approach.

Tell them that the owner is thankful for their interest and appreciates they are in a good position to buy, however, they felt their property was worth more.

Then give three reasons why this is. For example:

1. The last flat that sold in the block achieved a higher sale price, even though it was smaller.
2. They have several other viewings lined up and are confident there is demand for their property.
3. They are not in a hurry to sell and can wait for a better offer.

Point out that they still considered the offer and are motivated to sell, so they would be willing to accept an offer for, say, £10,000 more.

And then STOP TALKING once again and wait for feedback. Let them air their thoughts and encourage them to think about improving their position.

Continue with this formula of presenting counter offers until an agreement is reached. Sometimes, it may take several days or weeks to negotiate a sales price and allow for both parties to find a comfortable place within the boundaries of the deal. If a deal isn't reached, you must ensure both parties leave the process on a positive basis, as you never know when there may be a new opportunity to strike it again. As frustrating as it may be not to reach a deal, stay professional and polite and over time you will find this works in your favour. Your vendor will recognise that you have a strategy in place for achieving the best possible price, and a week or two later they may agree to accept the figure they previously turned down.

With lettings offers, it's often a much faster process. If the letting is not agreed within 24 to 36 hours, one of the parties involved is likely to move on. The main sticking points for negotiating lettings deals tend to be that the tenant is asking for work to be done to the property before moving in or has put in a request for certain furniture. Alternatively, there may be concerns about the tenant's financial status and ability to pay the rent. Take advice from your manager on these points, but use the same structure as above in terms of presenting your offers. You will be much more likely to get cooperation from all parties.

One final tip at this stage: always be complimentary. Tell the owner that the applicant really loves the property.

Meanwhile, tell the applicant that the owner feels they would be an excellent buyer/tenant and would like to sell/let the property to them. This simple gesture will greatly enhance the level of goodwill between the parties. It is your job to create a positive environment to facilitate the deal being agreed.

Once you have agreed a deal, you will be launched into the process of progressing the sale or letting to the point of the applicant moving into the property. There are agencies that will hand this over to a team of deal progressors, but for the majority of offices this role will stay with the negotiator who agreed the deal.

Sales progression basics

In a very brief summary, sales progression refers to the following stages in the sales process:

1) Agreeing the sale, collecting ID from the parties to the sale and ensuring there are signed agency terms and conditions from the owner, along with a completed PMA form.

2) Recommending a good quality firm of solicitors to each party, and sending out a memorandum of sale (this is a document that lists all parties to the sale and their solicitors).

3) Encouraging the buyer to book in any surveys or mortgage valuations required (ideally, they should take

place in the two weeks following the sale being agreed), and to instruct their solicitor to order any searches as early as possible.

4) Ensuring the owner completes and returns the relevant property information forms in a timely fashion.

5) Taking care of any renegotiations that arise following survey results and the arrival of the management information pack (if leasehold).

6) Encouraging all parties to proactively work towards exchange of contracts and negotiating a completion date.

7) The agent's work is effectively complete upon the exchange of contracts (when both parties to the sale sign a binding contract with a completion date and the buyer pays a deposit). At this point, the agent sends their commission invoice to the vendor's solicitor. This is usually paid direct to the agents by the solicitor from the proceeds of the sale.

8) Completion is when the solicitor acting for the vendor receives the money from the buyer's solicitors. When they have received all the money and 'completed' the transaction, they will call the agent's office to confirm it's Ok to release the keys to the property to the new owners. Don't hand out keys to a property without having been informed by the vendor's solicitor (not the buyer or their solicitor) that the property has completed.

Lettings progression basics

In a brief summary, lettings progression incorporates the following:

1) The tenant pays a holding deposit (usually non-refundable if they withdraw from the letting or fail their reference checks). They also pay a fee to cover referencing costs.

2) The references may be undertaken by a third party referencing agency or by the letting agent themselves. The negotiator oversees this process and takes ID from the tenants.

3) The owner needs to sign the agency terms and conditions, provide ID and proof of ownership of the property.

4) Assuming that the references are passed, the agent drafts the tenancy agreement, which the tenant signs and then pays the balance of the first month's rent (minus the holding deposit) and a deposit, which is usually one month or six weeks' rent. The agent normally executes the agreement on the move in date on behalf of the landlord and registers the deposit.

5) Before move in, the agent will also arrange an EPC and gas and electrical safety certificates, as well as any furnishing requests. If required, they will organise cleaning and any extra keys. They will book an inventory and check in to be undertaken by an independent check in clerk.

6) Depending on the contract terms, i.e. let only or managed, the agent may also handle the changeover of utility companies, register the deposit and ensure the tenant sets up their standing order for rent payment.

If the property is going to be managed by the agency, they will collect the rent on a monthly basis. Hence, the commission will be paid out of the monthly rent or taken from the first two months' rent, as it comes into the business. The negotiator will usually hand over to the property manager at move in.

If the property is rented on a 'let only' basis, often only the first month's rent will be retained to pay the agent's commission and an invoice will be issued if there is a remaining balance.

The first 10 to 15 deals you progress will be an uphill climb. After that time, you will speak confidently to your clients about the process, and your ability to deal with any crises as they arise will be greatly enhanced. Mastering the deal progression process will take time, but assuming that around 20% of all deals fall through before completion or move in, your ability to detect and resolve issues early on in the process will be essential to your long-term success in the industry. There will always be deals that fall apart no matter what you do. In these cases, the quicker you put the drama and disappointment behind you and move on to the next deal, the better. Dust yourself down, take on board any lessons learned and start working on your next offer. Don't spend the commission before it is securely in your bank account.

CHAPTER 7

SALES AND NEGOTIATION TRAINING AND QUALIFICATIONS

There are many routes you can take to improve your skills and knowledge and succeed as an estate agent. The majority of agents start their careers with very limited training and are effectively trained on the job. After your initial probation period has passed, your employer is likely to be more open to investing in further training and qualifications, as by this stage you will be considered a permanent employee.

There are many training options available to help you improve your knowledge and skills. These include online courses, group one-day sessions and the more rigorous, structured qualification schemes offered by the NAEA and ARLA. Both options have merit, depending on what is missing from your skillset. There is a huge benefit to taking time out of the office, mixing with agents from other companies and sharing a session on negotiation, sales progression or valuation skills. Within a very short period of time, you can gain a huge amount of highly applicable information designed specifically for your industry.

Most introductory and one-day courses cover a range of topics. Some are suitable for absolute beginners and others are for those looking to improve their negotiation or valuation skills, or their sales progression. On the lettings side, there is a considerable amount of landlord and tenant law relating to the day-to-day job. Taking a course that explains why a tenancy agreement contains certain clauses, the laws and regulations applying to tenant deposits and the basics of the eviction process can be extremely useful.

Most companies encourage junior lettings negotiators to work towards an ARLA qualification. ARLA offers introductory courses that provide a good overall grounding in the industry. For example, the ARLA 'Technical Award in Lettings and Property Management' involves working through a handbook requiring private study of around 60 hours. This is followed by sitting four multiple-choice exams conducted an at independent test centre. Once you have passed the tests, you are able to join the ARLA membership scheme and add the credentials MARLA (member of ARLA) after your name. Further training courses and levels can elevate your credentials to FARLA (fellow of ARLA), reflecting your knowledge and experience status. In an industry that isn't highly regarded by the public in general, these qualifications give huge credibility to your services and will help you to gain your client's trust and appreciation. Having a qualification will also make you and your company stand out from the crowd in what is a highly competitive industry. On the sales side, a similar technical award is available via the NAEA, leading to a MNAEA or FNAEA status. Often employers will view these qualifications as an essential part of their staff development and will pay for the course, give time off for study and award a bonus if the exams are passed first time around.

Taking a one-day training course can also help to break a negative sales cycle, i.e. if you've had a month of not hitting your target, a refresher course on sales techniques can really help you identify where you are going wrong, allowing you to refocus your activities in the right areas. Failing to hit your targets for a couple of months can really affect your motivation, changing your behaviour into acting 'desperate' (not least because your job is likely to be at risk by the third month). Someone who is flying high and hitting their sales targets acts, speaks and responds to clients in a very different manner to a negotiator who is desperate for a sale. Buyers and tenants can pick up on this positive or negative energy. Following a one-day course, it's easy to return to the office all fired up but then slip back into bad habits within a few days. So, when you return make sure you have a quick meeting with your manager, agree a method of monitoring your use of the new knowledge and have a follow-up meeting after five to seven days. If you manage to use your newly-gained habits for at least five days in a row, you'll be much more likely to continue to use them in the long-term.

One-day courses are available for more experienced negotiators. They may be focused on advanced negotiation skills, as well as leasehold or commercial property lease law. If you are aspiring towards a managerial position, it's a good idea to invest some time into developing your managerial skills, as the skillset and mindset of a good manager are different to those of a good negotiator. Good management skills can be developed over time, but they don't come naturally to most negotiators. You can improve your chances of promotion by demonstrating that you have invested time and energy into preparing for the role. A basic awareness of recruitment and employment law is also highly useful if you are going to become a manager.

CHAPTER 8

LONG-TERM CAREER PATHS AND RELATED INDUSTRIES

There are several routes to developing a successful career in estate agency. Most entrants into the industry start at junior negotiator-level and then work their way up. It's very unlikely that you will be employed as a branch manager without any prior experience of the industry, even if you have a high level of sales experience in a comparable industry.

In most offices, you'll find that you won't be the 'new person' for very long. One staff member will typically leave the branch every six to 12 months. It's generally cheaper to recruit a junior negotiator than it is to bring in a senior negotiator, and consequently an opportunity for progression will arise for most team members when a colleague leaves the company. Three to four years with the same agency is a relatively long period in the industry. The larger, more established agencies, such as Knight Frank and Savills, tend to retain staff for longer periods, and there is less seat hopping amongst prime central

London agents in comparison to those in suburban areas. This is because 'connections' and client relationships are a vital part of the job, with less clients being transient in comparison to the wider marketplace. Non-compete clauses within employment contracts will also prevent agents from moving to the competitor's office next door. Hence, there will be less flexibility to move jobs if you are working in a prime central London location.

A typical career path for a junior negotiator is as follows:

6 to 12 months as a junior negotiator.

12 months to 2 years as a negotiator.

2 years as a senior negotiator or assistant valuer (perhaps covering valuations when the office manager is away).

5 to 6 years minimum experience before promotion to branch manager.

5 to 10 years as a branch manager before promotion to director or area director level, if you are in a larger chain.

If the agency is relatively small, promotion opportunities are likely to come as team members leave or if the company is expanding. Otherwise, after two to three years with the same agency, if no promotion opportunities exist, it will be necessary to change agencies. The larger ones will consequently have a greater scope to retain and develop their staff than the smaller offices, as a greater number of roles will come up every year within the same organisation.

Likewise, if no opportunities exist to progress to director level once you have been a manager for some years, you may decide to start your own agency.

In both these cases, you will need to consider your notice period and any non-compete clauses that exist within your employment contract. These could range from one to three months' notice and prevent you from working for an agency that operates in the same postcode or within a certain radius of the office. The basic premise of the clause is that when you start to work for an agency, you will have access to its clients and database. Without a non-compete clause, you could take the client list to a competitor and steal business from your previous employer. If the clause covers too wide an area, it generally won't be enforceable. A well-written contract with a non-compete clause of 12 months within the same postcode(s) generally will be enforceable by law. Breaching your contract and starting work with a competitor next door will almost certainly result in legal action by your former employer. However, you have a right to carry on your trade and consequently, the non-compete clause needs to be specific and deemed fair in order for it to be upheld.

Related industries

There are a number of complementary careers within the industry that can be of interest to experienced agents. For example, property surveying would require two to three years of full-time study if you wanted to convert to this industry (or less if you already have a relevant qualification). Surveying requires higher qualification levels than estate agency, but employment opportunities are relatively abundant and the job is likely to reduce the number of evening and weekend hours required. A background in estate agency will be well regarded as a basis for entering the industry due to its high level of relevance with regards to valuing properties.

New homes

If you have traditional estate agency experience, the new homes industry is another area that's relatively easy to transition to. The term 'new homes' covers two types of transactions. If a property is sold 'off plan' this means it hasn't yet been built and the buyer selects their plot from an architect's model and sales brochure. A new build property is one that has been recently constructed, but not yet lived in. New homes agents also work with developers who convert existing buildings into new flats and houses.

The skills required for new homes sales are slightly

different to traditional estate agency in several areas. For example, rather than multiple owners each selling one property, you have one owner selling several properties that are likely to be very similar in terms of design, price, layout, etc.

The beauty of this is that you are given a list of prices and a set of plans and you sell the same 'product' again and again. You act for one vendor and negotiate on their behalf, often developing a long-term relationship with them. In traditional estate agency, you have the complication of many different properties, each with different work required. Some will have different lease terms, some will be in a chain and some will have legal issues, and so on. This is challenging but interesting work.

Conversely, dealing with new homes is much simpler and much more repetitive, with the advantage of selling a fixed range of properties, which usually have a 10-year building guarantee. If it's a flat a modern lease will be granted and usually the buyer won't need a surveyor to visit the property to look at the structure. In theory, therefore, it can be a much simpler transaction than selling an older property.

New homes sales have a typical cycle and there is a very heavy emphasis on marketing, networking and 'launching' the properties. This starts with a preparation phase, where the interior specifications are created and the outline pricing of the scheme is established. Then you have the scheme prelaunch, where investors and larger investment groups are invited to preview the plans. Often, bulk sales to the larger investor groups will be agreed before the public launch. A lead up to the main launch will go on for six weeks to six months. During this period, lots of marketing activities online and in the press will take place, inviting prospective buyers to register for the launch. At the main launch, the majority of the scheme or the first phase of the scheme (if multi-phase) will be put on sale to the general public (normally there is a drinks event with a show home and the opportunity for deposits to be taken). This is followed by several months or years of progressing those clients to completion once the properties are built.

Assuming you work within the new homes department of a large agency or directly for the developer, there will frequently be periods of time when you are waiting for the next scheme to launch. Consequently, your workload and earning potential will reduce considerably. Equally, you may be continually launching multiple schemes at any given time.

Most new homes schemes have a marketing suite on site. As the scheme is completed, your place of work is likely to change, depending on where the new scheme is located. So you would need to be comfortable with your place of work changing on a regular basis.

Crucially, whilst you may receive a retainer or a higher base salary and a lower commission rate compared to a typical high street agent, the majority of your commission will be paid upon completion of the build. Therefore, if you are selling off plan in a scheme with a two-year build timeframe, you will be waiting a long time to receive your commission. If you are considering a new homes job then you should ensure that you understand the typical payment timeframes on your sales.

There are superb career prospects within new homes, as successful agents often work with the same developer over a number of years. The launch of a new scheme is always a very exciting time, and its completion can also be a very satisfying process.

PRS sector

The private rented sector is, at the time of writing, a newly developing segment of the industry. It refers to institutional investment into new build accommodation, which is specifically destined to deliver homes to professional, long-term tenants in the private rental sector. There are numerous established schemes already, and many more in the pipeline, which are currently in the investment or construction phase. The buildings are specifically constructed or converted to accommodate a target market of young professionals who are increasingly opting to rent long-term rather than to buy their own home. Many of the schemes are located in commutable locations to major cities. The investors acquire the building and then use a management company to run it, which includes finding tenants and arranging and managing the tenancies. Other investors maintain the building and manage the tenancies in-house.

This is a relatively new concept for the UK market, but it's frequently seen in the US and elsewhere in Europe. Over the next five to 10 years, it's likely that a significant number of jobs will be created within this field.

Commercial property

Working as a commercial estate agent is significantly different to working as a residential one, however, it still requires some of the same skills. Rather than selling or letting residential property, a commercial agent works with retail units, restaurant and bar premises, warehouses and sites for redevelopment. The day-to-day work involves marketing commercial premises that are available to let and buy on websites such as estatesgazette.com, visiting sites with potential tenants and buyers and searching for premises and sites for retained clients. A retained client is typically an existing business that is searching for new premises in order to expand. The agent is paid a retainer fee to go and search for suitable premises and they are paid a commission if they are successful in negotiating a lease or purchase for that client. Many of the large chains in the UK work with smaller commercial agents, so you could find yourself negotiating with Starbucks for a new coffee shop or Tesco for a new supermarket site. Land sales and sites for redevelopment frequently form part of the workload, although land sales can also be considered as a standalone profession. Many entrants into the market will have completed some formal education in surveying, estate management or commercial law. However, it's possible to make the transition into commercial property from a residential agency background and work your way up within the industry. Many commercial agents work regularly with auctioneers, which is another varied and interesting career option within the property industry.

Like many industries, economic conditions can greatly affect the commercial property sector, and it can be particularly badly hit during times of uncertainty, as businesses stop expanding or close down and developers stop building. In positive market conditions, the job can be extremely diverse and rewarding and offers a good mix of office-based work and site visits, along with a decent work-life balance, as weekend and evening viewings are not generally required.

Property development and buy-to-let investment

Another career route that estate agents often follow is that of a property developer or buy-to-let investor. After a couple of years within the estate agency industry, you will understand the local marketplace and start to identify good opportunities for your own long-term financial benefit. After all, you'll have an insider's view to the local marketplace. You will know what sells, what lets, what is to be avoided and where the best development opportunities or rental returns can be found.

Many property professionals utilise their knowledge to develop their own buy-to-let investment portfolio, or they choose to become a part-time or full-time developer. Both of these activities can be highly profitable, although they also have the potential to be high risk and may not offer the same regularity of income as full-time employment. There is no doubt that estate agency experience offers an excellent grounding for success in these areas, as well as putting you in contact with builders, solicitors and mortgage brokers.

The typical career trajectory of a successful estate agent may resemble one of the following pathways:

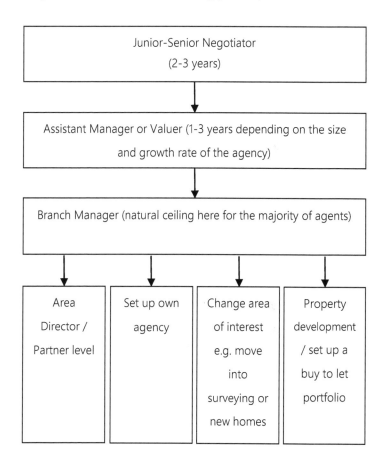

CONCLUSION

Despite the negative public opinion with regards to the average high street estate agent, the majority of agents find their career extremely interesting, challenging and ultimately highly rewarding, both in terms of personal satisfaction and income potential. Every single agent will recall the first property they ever sold or let, their viewing mishaps and their favourite and least-liked vendors and buyers. When asked to cite their favourite parts of the job, the majority of agents will tell you they love the variety and the fact that every day is different. They also may love seeing special or interesting properties and thrive on being out and about meeting people and viewing their homes. They might also find huge satisfaction in helping someone to find their new home, or deliver a great price for the owner. Most agents really love their job and choose to stay within the industry for many years.

Equipped with the knowledge contained within the preceding chapters, you should now have a realistic view of whether estate agency is for you. If you do decide to take your first steps into the industry, you can be confident that it will offer you an interesting and exciting career.

Printed in Great
Britain
by Amazon